GRAND CONCOURSE

GRAND CONCOURSE

⊰ A PLAY ⊱

HEIDI SCHRECK

NORTHWESTERN UNIVERSITY PRESS

EVANSTON, ILLINOIS

Northwestern University Press
www.nupress.northwestern.edu

Printed in the United States of America

10   9   8   7   6   5   4   3   2   1

ISBN 978-0-8101-3257-3 (paper)
ISBN 978-0-8101-3269-6 (e-book)

Cataloging-in-Publication Data are available from the Library of Congress.

♾ The paper used in this publication meets the minimum requirements of the American National Standard for Information Sciences—Permanence of Paper for Printed Library Materials, ANSI Z39.48-1992.

For Sherry Chastain Schreck

CONTENTS

Grand Concourse premiered Off-Broadway at Playwrights Horizons (the Peter Jay Sharp Theater) in New York City in October 2014. It was directed by Kip Fagan, with scenic design by Rachel Hauck, costume design by Jessica Pabst, lighting design by Matt Frey, and sound design by Leah Gelpe. The production stage manager was Sunneva Stapleton. The play, by Heidi Schreck, was developed with support of the Roe Green Award at Cleveland Play House and was first developed by the Cape Cod Theatre Project. It was also supported by the Tow Foundation Residency Program and the Edgerton Foundation New American Play Award. *Grand Concourse* was a 2015 Susan Smith Blackburn Award Finalist.

The cast of the New York production was as follows:

Shelley . . . . Quincy Tyler Bernstine
Emma . . . . Ismenia Mendes
Oscar. . . . . Bobby Moreno
Frog. . . . . Lee Wilkof

GRAND CONCOURSE

SETTING

A gleaming industrial kitchen in a Bronx church.

CHARACTERS

Shelley, late thirties
In charge of the kitchen for fifteen years. Catholic nun and former high school basketball star.

Emma, nineteen
Rainbow-colored hair. Loves horror movies. Recently dropped out of college.

Oscar, late twenties or early thirties
Security guard working his way through community college. Completed a year of dental school in the Dominican Republic.

Frog, fifties or sixties
Homeless former hippie and academic. Writes joke books.

NOTE:
In the text of the play, line breaks indicate a shift in thought and do not necessarily demand a pause. Actors should feel free to play around with the rhythms of the spoken word and to make choices about punctuation.

Dialogue frequently overlaps, and a slash (/) indicates where the next speaker begins.

PROLOGUE

[*The sound of microwave buttons being pushed.* SHELLEY *stands in front of the microwave.*]

SHELLEY:
Uh

[*She clears her throat.*]

Sorry I'm stuck I'm stuck uh
Why don't I start
I'll just start
Uh
I pray for all people
For all places where there is war or famine
I pray for our community

[*Long beat.*]

(. . . Justice for immigrants)

[*Long beat.*]

Sorry wow I'm so sorry
I'll keep working on this

[*The microwave beeps.*]

SCENE ONE

SHELLEY:
They can be high or drunk they can be falling down
as long as they aren't violent
If they're violent you call Oscar
The guys love him he's Dominican
He speaks Spanish and English and something else
He can fix things too
Officially he's maintenance
but he got roped into being our muscle
It's a long story and I don't want to scare you

[SHELLEY *dumps several cups of barley into a pot of water as she talks.*]

Since this might be their main nutrition
we use beans, barley, brown rice, whole grains
we change it up
All the veggies are in this big fridge
zucchini, carrots, sometimes other squashes, no onions
Onion allergies are apparently on the rise
Here's a knife did you wash your hands?

EMMA:
No

SHELLEY:
Use that sink the water is brown in the other one
for some reason
and then put on a pair of gloves
You want to change your gloves often
touch the garbage—change your gloves
start a new vegetable—change your gloves
actually that's probably overkill but I'm a clean freak so I'm gonna
make you do it anyway
Potatoes are in these boxes here
You can use as many potatoes as you want
they're good filler

EMMA:
No meat?

SHELLEY:
Oh yeah we serve steak and also we have Lobster Fridays
no it's too expensive
Dinners are fancier but
this meal is just to get people through the day
We get a small crowd for lunch
mostly men
so in terms of interaction the main thing is to have boundaries
You can joke around with the guys
but don't let them own you and don't give them money

EMMA:
. . . OK

[SHELLEY *digs in the bottom drawer of the refrigerator.*]

SHELLEY:
Oh man Luis got these honking carrots again

[*She emerges with a bag of gigantic carrots.*]

You'll have to use the big knife
try not to cut your finger
I cut my fingers a couple of times a month
(I'm trying to be more mindful)

[*She surveys the vegetables.*]

This here is what I call Shelley's famous
barley carrot zucchini potato soup

[*Beat. She takes in* EMMA *for the first time.*]

. . . How did you find us anyway?

EMMA:
The Internet

SHELLEY:
You were Googling soup kitchens or

EMMA:
Yeah no soup kitchens
I thought if I gave back in some way
if I did something for other people
I thought it would help

SHELLEY:
Help what

EMMA:
Oh well them I guess the people who need help
and also me

SHELLEY:
How old are you?

EMMA:
Nineteen

SHELLEY:
Are you in college?

EMMA:
I was I dropped out I got kicked out

[*Beat.*]

SHELLEY:
Do you want to chop some carrots?

EMMA:
. . . Sure

[*They start chopping.*]

Are a lot of them falling down drunk
the guys who come here

SHELLEY:
No most of our guests are very polite
especially the regulars
But you do have to be careful
because any one of them could snap
There's this one guy Frog
He comes every day and he'll try to sell you these joke books

[*A rock hits the window. They both jump.* SHELLEY *runs to the doorway.*]

EMMA:	SHELLEY [*shouting*]:
Jesus	Oscar!
(sorry)	Hey Oscar!

SHELLEY:
It's shatterproof don't worry
Oscar!
It's kids they think it's funny
Oscar will scare them away
OSCAR!

[OSCAR *enters.*]

OSCAR:
Hey where's my sandwich

SHELLEY:
It's those P.S. 96 kids throwing rocks again
Can you go outside and scare them

OSCAR:
Yeah but then I need my sandwich

[*To* EMMA] Hi

[*To* SHELLEY] She's cute
I mean you're my true love Shelley
You're my love for all space and time
but she's cute too

SHELLEY:
Hurry up

OSCAR:
OK but don't worry
ladies
I AM COMING BACK

[OSCAR *exits.*]

SHELLEY:
He's uh
He brings a lot of energy to the place

[*Small beat.* SHELLEY *looks around the kitchen.*]

Uh
OK
After this we'll clean the dining room
sweep up
The tables can be sprayed down with that
Stuff
under there
And there are brooms and mops and things in the hallway
The janitors have already been in
but I always do a final go over

EMMA:
Do you use organic cleaning products

SHELLEY:
Ha
No

EMMA:
I'm sorry it's just I'm allergic
to chemical cleaners

[*Beat.*]

SHELLEY:
I guess you're in charge of the sweeping

[OSCAR *reenters.*]

OSCAR:
OK ladies they're gone
I threatened to cut their fingers off with these pliers
now I need my sandwich

SHELLEY:
Good work

OSCAR:
Does that mean you'll see a movie with me

SHELLEY:
Ha ha ha here

OSCAR:
How come it's always Roast Beef

SHELLEY:
Because Roast Beef is your favorite

OSCAR [*as he eats*]:
Oh yeah

[*He looks* EMMA *up and down as he eats his sandwich.*]

You really are pretty
Like a Greek goddess what's-her-name Icarus

SHELLEY:
Don't play dumb Icarus was a boy
He knows that he goes to City College
Don't play dumb you think it's charming but it's not

OSCAR:
Oh right Icarus is the guy whose wings melted
I forgot I did I forgot!
I meant the goddess who's

Iris
the Rainbow one

SHELLEY:
Why because of her hair?

OSCAR:
Yeah I like that
what you've done with your hair
Very creative

EMMA:
Oh yeah it's
I was hating myself
and I thought maybe if I changed my hair
I wouldn't notice it was me . . .

OSCAR:
OK so you're crazy
No that's OK that's hot
I mean it's like I'm gonna stay away
but you're still hot
You know
From way back here from a distance

SHELLEY:
Be nice Oscar

EMMA:
I don't actually hate myself all the time, Oscar
I was just having a bad day but I feel a lot better now that I'm

[*She makes a goddessy gesture.*]

. . . Iris

OSCAR:
Heh
Yeah
It's a full moon tonight Sister Shelley
don't get too wild
The biggest full moon in twenty years so

[*Pause.*]

... watch out

[OSCAR *exits.* SHELLEY *and* EMMA *chop.*]

EMMA:
He's cute

[*They chop.*]

Sorry you're not supposed to notice that right

SHELLEY:
How would I not notice that

EMMA:
Yeah but aren't you supposed to
detach from those feelings or

SHELLEY:
No not from feelings no

[*They chop.*]

... Just from outcomes

[*After a bit.*]

EMMA:
Sorry if I'm being nosy
but how come you don't wear a head thing

SHELLEY:
A lot of us stopped doing that in the seventies

[*They chop.*]

Although some of the younger nuns
are bringing it back
I have no idea why
A group of them play basketball across the street
in their habits

EMMA:
Whoa

[SHELLEY *chops rather violently.*]

SHELLEY:
Yeah half-court ball because they can't move very fast
I mean I love basketball
but I am not playing in a dress
Go ahead and dump the vegetables into the pot

[EMMA *dumps all of her vegetables into the pot.* SHELLEY *does the same.*]

And now we put the lid on

[SHELLEY *puts the lid on. She gestures to a bunch of cleaning supplies in the corner.*]

Why don't you grab that broom and I'll show you the dining area

EMMA:
OK wait let me

[EMMA *goes to her bag and gets out an allergy mask. She puts it on.* SHELLEY *looks at her.*]

SHELLEY:
Super

[*They exit.*]

SCENE TWO

[FROG *enters. He goes to the big fridge, opens it, and starts snacking on vegetables with his head inside the fridge.* EMMA *enters, carrying the broom and dustpan. She is still wearing the allergy mask. She sees* FROG.]

EMMA:
Oscar
Oscar

FROG:
Hey whoa calm / down

EMMA:
OSCAR

FROG:
Whoa it's me it's Frog
Calm down
Are you / new

EMMA:
You're Frog

FROG [*obviously*]:
Yeah

EMMA:
I'm sorry sir
Frog
You need to wait out in the cafeteria
We'll be serving lunch in a few minutes

FROG:
Yeah but I'm a snacker

EMMA:
OK but you can't / be in here

FROG:
Would you like to buy a joke

[*Beat.*]

EMMA:
How much

FROG:
One joke is a quarter
or I can sell you the whole book for a buck
There's at least thirty jokes in the book
It's a much better deal

EMMA:
Oh uh

FROG:
Why didn't the chicken cross the road

EMMA:
I don't know
Why didn't the chicken cross / the

FROG:
No training

[*Beat.* EMMA *starts laughing.*]

You see
Give me a dollar
You need this book

EMMA:
I'm sorry I don't have any cash / on me

FROG:
You can have it for free I trust you

EMMA:
Oh no / I couldn't

FROG:
Take it
Take it

EMMA:
Thank you OK wait I actually do have a dollar in my bag
I don't know why I said I didn't

[*She gives him a dollar and puts the book in her bag.*]

FROG:
You won't be sorry I'm a fortune-teller too I come from
A long line of Gypsies
Of Romani sorry the Romani people
so I can see your future
And you have a lot of laughs coming your way

[SHELLEY *enters with an armful of dirty serving platters.*]

SHELLEY:
Hey Frog you know you can't be in here

FROG:
I can go anywhere I want Shelley

[*He turns back to* EMMA.]

For a while I was in exile they banished me
The cops picked me up in Eugene, Oregon
and instead of taking me to jail
They gave me a one-way ticket to Berkeley, California
"Because it's always warm in Berkeley"

SHELLEY:
It's not always warm / in Berkeley

FROG:
Warmer than / here

SHELLEY:
Frog, go get in line

FROG:
Berkeley sucks too many bums

SHELLEY:
Frog

FROG [*to* EMMA]:
Shattuck Street—you ever been
Shitsuck Street
Bums puking all over your shoes
Stupid cracked-out hippies

SHELLEY:
I'm calling security

[FROG *is gone.*]

Did you buy one of his books

EMMA:
. . . Yeah

SHELLEY:
OK then you're contributing to his alcoholism

EMMA:
It was a dollar

SHELLEY:
A dollar toward his death
Don't encourage him he's a manipulator

EMMA:
He seems so nice

SHELLEY:
Yeah well he got in a fight once
right out there on the corner of 196th and Grand Concourse
Broke a guy's collarbone
He just snapped OK any of them can snap
so you need to pay attention when / I

EMMA:
I have cancer

SHELLEY:
What

EMMA:
That's why I have to wear this mask
I know you think I'm wimpy
I could tell by the way you were looking at me

in this mask
but I'm not a wimp I have cancer

[*Beat.*]

SHELLEY:
I'm sorry I had no idea

EMMA:
It's OK it's not your / fault

SHELLEY:
I'm so sorry what kind of

EMMA:
Leukemia
The kid kind so that's lucky

SHELLEY:
Are you sure you're all right / to

EMMA:
Yes yes I'm fine
It's good for me to get out and do stuff
as long as I'm careful
I'm sorry I should / have told you

SHELLEY:
No no please you have nothing to be sorry for
we're happy that you're here

[OSCAR *enters.*]

OSCAR:
Hey are we on schedule

EMMA:
That was a very poor response time Oscar

OSCAR:
Hey crazy
There's a huge line out there
Is that last pot ready to run

SHELLEY:
Uh
Yes I think we're ready

[*She picks up the pot of soup with pot holders and hands it to* OSCAR. OSCAR *takes the pot and ushers the ladies out in front of him.*]

OSCAR:
Let's get it moving ladies
Right this way
Watch your backs 'cause it's hot behind

[*They exit.*]

OSCAR [*as he is disappearing*]:
Showtime

SCENE THREE

[EMMA *lugs in two giant recycling bags filled with paper plates. She is wearing her mask. She unlocks the back door, looks around, and tosses them into the cans.* EMMA *shuts the door quickly and locks it. She takes off her mask. She's exhausted.*]

[OSCAR *enters carrying the giant soup pot.*]

OSCAR:
You hungry
You want some of this leftover soup

EMMA:
No thanks

OSCAR:
Seriously you should eat that takes a lot of energy
and you're not even good at it yet
Wait till you get to my level
I always have a big bowl of soup afterwards because I deserve it
You wanna join me

EMMA:
Uh

OSCAR:
C'mon a little fellowship here

[*He ladles out two bowls of soup and puts them in the microwave.*]

You mind if I nuke 'em?

EMMA:
. . . No

OSCAR:
Hey are you OK

EMMA:
Yeah yeah I'm
That was a little overwhelming

OSCAR:
First time can be rough
You can't let 'em wear you out
Gotta protect yourself

EMMA:
That's a lot of I don't know
Need

OSCAR:
Desperation man that's desperation

EMMA:
I feel like I'm covered in gunk now
I feel desperate too like it's contagious
I think I'm gonna go home and take a shower
and then maybe go to Sephora try out some new products

OSCAR:
Oh man
Sephora
My girlfriend spends her whole paycheck there
then I gotta pay for her to eat

EMMA [*digging in her bag*]:
Yeah I get it
It makes you feel really good about yourself
Here I'll show you
This is a brand called Benefit the packaging is really pleasing
Look at this
This is a whole kit for your eyes

OSCAR:
Oh yeah that is pretty

EMMA:
Right?
This covers up your dark circles
And this you can use to put a little shimmer under the brow bone
And here I'm going to line my eyes

[*He heads to the microwave to prepare the soup as she makes her eyes a little more glamorous.*]

OSCAR:
Hey do what you gotta do
Just don't poke your eye out
My sister almost did that once had to wear a patch
She worked it though
still had dudes asking her out
Soup's ready

EMMA:
Just a second

[OSCAR *brings over two steaming bowls of soup and utensils.*]

OSCAR:
Wow you look good that stuff really works

EMMA:
This is my Buxom lip gloss and plumper
It tingles

[*She smoothes the lip gloss on her lips.*]

It actually makes my lips plumper
that's why it stings
Like a bee has actually stung my lip
Do they look plumper

[*Beat.*]

OSCAR:
I dunno

[*He starts eating the soup. As he's eating he sort of mumbles.*]

I know that personally
I would not want that crap in my soup

[*She laughs. She takes one of the napkins and wipes off the lip gloss. She starts eating the soup.*]

EMMA:
Do you ever work here at night

OSCAR:
I do sometimes yeah
On Fridays

EMMA:
So like this Friday

OSCAR:
Uh no I'm off this Friday

EMMA:
Is it scary

OSCAR:
Nah
There's guys hanging around
but they're just looking for handouts or a warm place to sleep

EMMA:
Right but are there ghosts

OSCAR:
Uh no I don't think so

EMMA:
It would be cool to spend the night in a spooky old church
I like to get freaked out

[*They eat. The silence goes on a little too long.*]

OSCAR:
So you
I guess you like horror movies then

EMMA:
Oh yeah
I'm not like most girls I fucking love horror movies
The Omen is my favorite
Old Timey horror

OSCAR:
That's cool my girl is not into them at all
My girlfriend
Rosa
She makes me go to girl movies

EMMA:
Some night I'm gonna show up here
and scare the shit out of you

OSCAR:
Uh no
No
I don't think you should do that

EMMA:
Better stay on your toes

[SHELLEY *enters with an armload of tablecloths and napkins. She shoves them into a hamper as she talks.*]

SHELLEY:
Oscar will you put the chairs away after you eat
Those nice lady volunteers just bailed
Rafa told them he had lice

OSCAR:
Sure

EMMA:
Wait which one is Rafa

OSCAR:
The guy with the nasty hair down to his butt

[SHELLEY *grabs a mop and bucket from the closet.*]

EMMA:
He has lice

OSCAR: SHELLEY:
No   Probably

OSCAR:
No he doesn't
He was just messing with the ladies

SHELLEY:
I bet he does have lice but that doesn't mean
we can all run screaming back to wherever
Riverdale
I'm so sick of volunteers

OSCAR:
Shelley

SHELLEY [*to* EMMA]:
Oh no I'm so sorry I don't mean you
You were wonderful the guests loved you

[EMMA *beams.*]

OSCAR:
Oh man look at that smile
You made this girl's day Shelley

[As SHELLEY is exiting]

Hey what about me I work hard too

SHELLEY:
You're getting paid

[SHELLEY is gone.]

EMMA:
Shouldn't we go help her

OSCAR:
No way she never stops working
She's got superpowers from God
I'm telling you she comes in at 6 A.M.
So she can clean up *after* the janitors
You try and keep up you'll never get outta here

EMMA:
Right but I don't want her to be mad at me

OSCAR:
Who Shelley no way she forgives everybody
Don't worry about it
Just eat your soup that's my advice

EMMA:
Yeah OK

[*They eat.*]

Hey this is actually pretty good

OSCAR:
Yeah it's not bad for bum soup right
Soup desperadoes
Could use some more pepper

[*He grabs some pepper and shakes it in his soup.*]

EMMA:
I'll take some in my soup too

OSCAR:
Sure

[*He reaches his hand out to give her the pepper.* EMMA *doesn't take the pepper.*]

EMMA:
Go ahead

[*Beat.*]

OSCAR:
You want me to put the pepper in your soup

EMMA:
Yeah

[*Beat.*]

OSCAR:
Like I'm a waiter?

EMMA:
Yeah
Like you're a *waiter*

[*Beat.*]

[OSCAR *reluctantly peppers her soup.*]

SCENE FOUR

[*The sound of microwave buttons being pushed.* SHELLEY *stands in front of the microwave.*]

SHELLEY:
Forgive me but it feels pointless lately
keeping these people alive with so little
And I think I have skills that might be more useful
I'm not even a great cook so
I've been thinking lately should I go back to school
Become a
. . . a lawyer
I could probably do more good as a lawyer
My mind is atrophying here
I used to think the conversations I had with these people
were deeper and more meaningful
than those I have with my peers
Forgive me they are my peers too
I know their value I do I'm just grumpy
I know I would feel worse if I had to spend my days
with a bunch of jerk lawyers like my dad

[*Beat.*]

He's uh
He's still hanging on and I know
I need to reach out
. . . To forgive

[*She sighs.*]

But sometimes I wish he would just hurry up and die
Forgive me

[EMMA *enters and stands in the doorway.*]

I know that you are looking at me with gentleness
I know that whatever my faults
You will continue to look at me with gentleness

[SHELLEY *crosses herself.*]

Amen

[*The microwave beeps.* SHELLEY *turns to see* EMMA.]

EMMA:
Oscar let me in I hope that's OK

SHELLEY:
Emma
Hi
Are you on the schedule

EMMA:
No but I had blood work up the street so
I thought I'd stop by
see if you and Oscar needed any help

SHELLEY:
Oh OK most volunteers don't come back the next day
so good for you
but we don't start serving till two and I uh
you know what come on in anyway I'm just planning the menu
Have you eaten yet

EMMA:
Not really

SHELLEY:
Why don't you sit down I'll make you a sandwich
Is Roast Beef OK it's all we've got

EMMA:
I love Roast Beef but I'm not hungry
I'm here to help

[SHELLEY *goes to the fridge.*]

SHELLEY:
Well you need to eat so I am making you this sandwich
And I am sticking it in the fridge for later
Don't let Oscar eat it
He could eat ten sandwiches at a time

EMMA:
Thank you

[SHELLEY *starts making* EMMA's *sandwich.*]

SHELLEY:
What you're going through
has gotta be tough
Do you have people taking care of you

EMMA:
Yeah my mom but she's driving me crazy
I mean I know she's worried but
I just want her to treat me like a normal person

SHELLEY:
. . . Sure

[EMMA *watches* SHELLEY *make the sandwich.* SHELLEY *smiles at her.*]

Hey guess what
One of our parishioners
donated a bunch of eggplant today
See that crate
Do you have any idea what to do with those

EMMA:
Not really

SHELLEY:
Yeah me either
We usually stick to the basics around here but
Sandwich!
I found this eggplant soup recipe on Epicurious
Maybe you can help me with that

EMMA:
Sure

[OSCAR *enters carrying a box of canned goods. He notices* EMMA.]

OSCAR [*to* EMMA]:
Oh wow she let you stay I guess she loves you

SHELLEY [*still holding up the eggplant*]:
Hey Oscar what do you call this in Spanish

OSCAR:
Eggplant I mean *berenjena*
Berenjenas

SHELLEY:
Do you know what the heck to do with it

OSCAR:
Yeah, you just scoop it out and fry the guts in a pan

[*He sets the box down, opens it, and starts stocking one of the shelves.*]

SHELLEY:
The guts

OSCAR:
Yeah it's delicious like mashed potatoes

SHELLEY:
Right but we have to put it in a soup

EMMA:
Duh

OSCAR:
OK well then you know what's delicious
is eggplant in a pork stew my sister makes that
Why don't you make that

SHELLEY:
It's lunch we can't afford pork

OSCAR:
OK but I'm saying I personally if it were up to me
I would chop it up and make a pork and eggplant stew
But that's me
can I get my sandwich

EMMA:
Here I got it

[EMMA *goes to the fridge, opens it, and pulls out a sandwich. As* SHELLEY *squints at the recipe,* EMMA *unwraps the sandwich. Looking right at* OSCAR, *she starts eating it.*]

SHELLEY:
So I just chunk it up, Oscar?

[OSCAR *is staring at* EMMA.]

Do I leave this skin on

OSCAR:
Yes yes you leave the skin on
because it has vitamins
This girl is eating my sandwich!

[EMMA *starts laughing.*]

EMMA:
I'm not I'm not this is my sandwich
Shelley made this for me
THIS IS MY SANDWICH

OSCAR:
Girl is crazy

[EMMA *takes out* OSCAR'*s sandwich.*]

EMMA [*laughing*]:
Dude here's your sandwich

[EMMA *is laughing almost hysterically now.* SHELLEY *is a little confused.*]

SHELLEY:
OK let's all just
calm down
Oscar we have a lot of work to do
And too many cooks in the kitchen so

OSCAR:
I didn't do anything she did it!

SHELLEY:
I'm just saying we've got to
Grapple
[*holding up the eggplant*]
with this

OSCAR:
I hear you Shelley I'm gonna leave you two alone
(go eat my sandwich)

[*He exits.* SHELLEY *looks at* EMMA.]

EMMA:
Sorry

SHELLEY:
. . . It's OK he was distracting us

EMMA:
Totally

[SHELLEY *is still holding the eggplant.*]

You want me to try?

SHELLEY:
Please

[EMMA *takes the eggplant and starts cutting it up slowly, but fairly confidently.* SHELLEY *watches her, impressed.*]

All right that's your job

[SHELLEY *goes to grab a bunch of potatoes.*]

EMMA:
So you like
pray to the microwave

SHELLEY:
What
Oh
No
Ha
No I don't pray to the
I don't worship the microwave

EMMA:
The microwave god

SHELLEY:
No no the microwave

[*Beat.*]

It's for keeping time I was timing my prayer

EMMA:
Why

SHELLEY:
Uh
I've been having a little trouble praying
Lately

EMMA:
Whoa you're a nun

SHELLEY:
Right but it's something I'm struggling with nevertheless

EMMA:
And the microwave helps

SHELLEY:
Well the timer helps
I've been forcing myself to pray for
One minute
I'm trying to work up to two
and eventually five

EMMA:
Whoa

SHELLEY:
Yep

[SHELLEY *starts chopping potatoes. They chop for a bit.*]

EMMA:
Do you like picture a face when you pray

SHELLEY:
No
I don't

EMMA:
When I was a kid we said that prayer
"If I should die before I wake
I pray the Lord my soul to take"
So I always pictured a monster with a giant mouth
waiting for me to die so he could eat my soul

[*They chop.* SHELLEY *doesn't quite know what to say. She clears her throat.*]

SHELLEY:
If you'd like to talk to someone
about praying
I'm sure Father Nolan would be happy / to

EMMA:
Ew no thanks

[*They keep chopping.*]

SHELLEY [*after a few moments*]:
Uh
When I first started learning to pray
I was taught to imagine a real person who loved me
Unconditionally
So I would just talk to my Grandma
she was crazy about me
and she was dead so she couldn't change her mind

[FROG *enters.*]

SHELLEY [*without looking up*]:
Frog
Out

[FROG *exits.*]

SCENE FIVE

[*Sounds of shuffling around in the dark. Muttering in Spanish. Sound of a woman laughing.*]

OSCAR:
What are you
What are you
Oh Jesus
What are you doing

[OSCAR *is breathing heavily.*]

Ta pasao
Tu ta pasao
Tu ta pasao

[OSCAR *comes. Beat.*]

Shit

SCENE SIX

[*Morning.* FROG *and* OSCAR *in the kitchen.* OSCAR *is making eggs.*]

FROG:
So after that
Let me say that I had also eaten many mushrooms
Purple heads so I should have been having Visions
but for some reason I wasn't
The experience it was
It was purely tactile
I might as well have eaten ecstasy
which is fine I love ecstasy
but I was looking for a transformational experience
and ecstasy does not transform
It keeps you solidly in this

[FROG *pats his belly.*]

So after that I had to quit there was no other choice

[*He pats his belly again.*]

Geez I'm getting fat all this soup

OSCAR:
You're not fat Papi

FROG:
Oh yeah

OSCAR:
You like the yolk hard or soft

FROG:
Oh hard as hard as you can get it
Otherwise I think about the dead baby chick
That's an embryo you know that's an abortion

OSCAR:
Hey come on

FROG:
I'm sorry my friend but that's what it is
I was a vegetarian for years
First just to piss off my parents but then I really meant it
And then I didn't eat anything at all for a whole month
Because I got to thinking that plants are alive too
I would eat some iceberg lettuce
feel it crunch between my teeth
hear the screams of pain
Carrot sticks were the worst
The sound they make oh man ahhhhh

[*He covers his ears for a second.*]

You know what I'm talking about?
Snapping carrot bones with your murderous teeth?

OSCAR:
Carrots don't have bones man

FROG:
Sure they do they've got a spine
You know that little inside tube of the carrot
You know the tube the delicate tube
that's the Spine and listen when you start to realize
that everything is alive
and trust me everything is alive
Then you start to realize you have a choice to make
You can either decide that you are a predator
no different than a lion or a
piranha
crushing life in your murderous teeth
or you can starve to death
That's your choice

[*Beat.*]

And it's bleak
It's a bleak choice
Look the sun is coming up
Love it
Love the sun
Love the sun
Is there coffee

OSCAR:
Yeah
You take milk sugar

FROG:
Oh no black
black black black

OSCAR:
Man I don't know how you can drink it without sugar

FROG:
Yeah well I'm epileptic and the sugar makes it worse
Epilepsy
you know what that is
"Epilepsia"

OSCAR:
Yeah OK

FROG:
I can say it five different languages just in case
When I was young I was a global adventurer
I've been all over Europe I've been to Africa
that big warm cradle
Also I wear this thing this necklace
tells people what my deal is
in case I flip out on a subway platform or on the sidewalk
That's another reason I quit the drugs
and the alcohol
You wouldn't know it but I actually take very good care of myself
You should tell Shelley tell her
tell her I'm not a drunk
Tell that Gargoyle I look out / for myself

OSCAR:
Here you go here's your eggs

[OSCAR *hands* FROG *a plate of eggs.*]

FROG:
Aren't you going to eat

OSCAR:
I can't I'm thinking of the baby chicks

FROG:
Well you're going to have to eat at some point
At some point you're going to have to make peace
with being a murderer

[FROG *eats his eggs with relish.* OSCAR *drinks coffee.*]

[FROG *makes growling noises.*]

OSCAR:
Frog cut it out

[FROG *continues to eat.*]

FROG:
Hey Oscar
Why did the boy drop his ice cream

OSCAR:
I don't know why

FROG:
Because he got hit by a truck

[*Beat.*]

OSCAR:
Man I'm sorry but I don't understand your jokes

FROG:
What are you talking about

OSCAR:
I don't know maybe it's my English

FROG:
Your English is perfect

OSCAR:
Jokes are the last thing you understand in another language
Sucks
I need special English as a Second Language jokes I guess

FROG:
Listen my friend my jokes don't make any sense
don't worry about it
Hey how's your girl
what's her name?

OSCAR:
Rosa

FROG:
Oh yeah Rosa I like her
How's she doing

OSCAR:
She's good
Oh
Yeah
Papi she's great she's
She wants me to marry her so I'm
working up to that

FROG:
What the hell does that mean

OSCAR:
Well I don't have the cash to provide for her right now
so it doesn't seem right to marry her
Once I get my degree I can get a better job / and

FROG:
What kind of job you gonna get
There are no jobs my friend don't delude yourself
There are no jobs
There are no jobs
Marry her now you guys can figure it out together
This is the twenty-first century you don't have to support her
In the twenty-first century men and women they support each other
You see:

[*He makes a gesture with his hands resembling "This is the church, this is the steeple."*]

I am holding you up while you are holding up me
It's fucking beautiful
The twenty-first century
The twenty-first century
Isn't this what you really want

[*He makes the gesture again.*]

This right here

OSCAR:
Yeah that sounds nice

FROG:
Oh it's nice it's nice

OSCAR:
You have a girl

FROG:
No no no no no
That's not my way Oscar

OSCAR:
You what gay Frog you

FROG:
All I'm going to say about this Oscar
Is that it is not my way
And then I'm going to leave you to draw
whatever conclusions you like
I'll tell you one thing though:
Unlike some people I am not a playa

[*Beat.*]

OSCAR:
Oh man what are you talking about / "playa"

FROG:
Well my friend I'm camping near the rectory now

OSCAR:
Frog you know you're not supposed to camp

FROG:
I know but I am
I am camping near the rectory and I saw
Oh yeah
Oh yeah
Round 3 A.M. I saw her come in
Oh yeah
and then later I saw her go out
Oh yeah

[*Beat.*]

You got something to say about that

OSCAR:
Shit

FROG:
Oh yeah

OSCAR:
She just showed up

FROG:
All her fault huh

OSCAR:
Yeah
Actually!
I was sleeping and I opened my eyes and
there she was right there front of me
I thought I was dreaming
Oh man c'mon it was a mistake
Let's forget about it I'm going to forget about it
I gotta headache now

FROG:
Yeah but did you have sex with her

OSCAR:
No no no I didn't I
I didn't have sex with her
She did it all without any help from me
I did nothing I didn't even touch her
She did it all and then she left it was like a dream
So you see I think technically I'm in the clear with Rosa because
One: We didn't technically have sex
And Two: I thought I was dreaming

[*Beat.*]

FROG:
Sweet dream

[OSCAR *nods.*]

SCENE SEVEN

[*In front of the microwave at 6 A.M.*]

SHELLEY:
I know you are asking me to go further here
To go the second mile
But I'm not sure what I have to offer this girl

[*Long beat.* SHELLEY *closes her eyes. She starts to pray more formally.*]

By your blessing give her strength and support her in her frailty
Free her from illness and restore her to health
So that in the sure knowledge of your goodness
She will gratefully bless your holy name

[SHELLEY *opens her eyes.*]

Give her more time here to know you
To know herself
Touch gently this life that you have created

[*She turns off the microwave.*]

SCENE EIGHT

[*The following week.* OSCAR *is eating his sandwich. He occasionally looks at the door, as if he's waiting for someone.* SHELLEY *is prepping the soup.*]

OSCAR:
You know I was gonna be a dentist right
I went back and did a year of training in the DR
but none of it counts here that's the problem
If I want to be a dentist here I've gotta start all over
And yeah I could go back to the DR
set up a clinic make a shitload of money
but I don't wanna go back there my life is here now
New York City is the new Dominican Republic

SHELLEY:
Can you grab me that pot from up there

OSCAR:
You know most fools in the DR think that New York City
IS America
Yeah
My cousin called last week
he said Oscar we're moving to New York City
and I said shit that's great news do you need a place to live
and he said no no no man we found a place
in Miami

SHELLEY:
Ha

OSCAR:
So one date Shelley what do you say?

SHELLEY:
Get back to work Oscar

OSCAR:
I'm teasing you!
I mean sometimes it's fun to think
Could I compete with God
And I think
Yeah

[SHELLEY *reacts.*]

I'm kidding!
C'mon I'm kidding I respect you
and also I love Rosa
I love Rosa you know I do

SHELLEY:
How is Rosa

OSCAR:
Oh she's good she's good
she's gotta new job
Yeah she's gonna be making more money than me
She's working at Macy's

SHELLEY:
That's great

OSCAR:
Hey when's that girl coming in again

SHELLEY:
Who
Emma

OSCAR:
Yeah she disappeared what's up with that

SHELLEY:
Uh
I'm not sure I haven't heard from her

OSCAR:
Oh really oh great cause she's crazy

SHELLEY:
Oscar stop it she has a lot going on right now

OSCAR:
She got a lot of problems huh rich girl problems

SHELLEY:
I don't think she's rich

OSCAR:
Between you and me I think girl's a crazy bitch

[SHELLEY *looks up, horrified.*]

Sorry!
Sorry I never use that word
I'm sorry Shelley will you forgive me

[*It's not clear whether* SHELLEY *will forgive him.*]

It's just there's something about her she freaks me out

SHELLEY:
You don't know anything about her

OSCAR:
Oh I know some things

SHELLEY:
You need to be kind to her do you hear me

OSCAR:
Not if she's bat-shit crazy I don't

SHELLEY:
Oscar shut up she's sick OK she's very / sick

OSCAR:
What do you mean she's sick

SHELLEY:
Never mind I don't know if I / should

OSCAR:
Yeah but wait is she like

[Beat.]

Is it contagious?

SHELLEY:
Oscar!

OSCAR:
Sorry I

SHELLEY:
No it's not contagious!

OSCAR:
OK sorry I'm just saying
she shouldn't be serving soup if she's gonna be infectious

SHELLEY:
What is with you Oscar

OSCAR:
I don't know!
Something
Something's up with me

SHELLEY:
Yeah

OSCAR [*after a moment*]:
Rosa and I are
We've been fighting all week and I don't know why
It's stressing me out
I'm sorry Shelley is that girl going to be OK

SHELLEY:
I don't know but she needs all the support we can give her

OSCAR:
I hear you

SHELLEY
Do you mind chopping some vegetables

OSCAR:
No way that's women's work
Ha I'm kidding
Here I'll do the carrots

[OSCAR *puts a pair of gloves on.*]

SHELLEY:
I'm supposed to have a volunteer coming
but apparently he's late

OSCAR:
Dude volunteer
Finally
Thank you God

[*They both chop fairly quickly.*]

Hey just so you know
Frog's camping in the rectory

SHELLEY:
What no he can't do that

OSCAR:
I know but he is
S'okay if I give him breakfast

SHELLEY:
Oscar he can't camp

OSCAR:
I know but is it OK if I feed him until he gets caught

[*She sighs.*]

SHELLEY:
Yes

OSCAR:
I knew you'd say yes
You nuns are sneaky
Sneaky for God

[*A rock hits the window.*]

SHELLEY:
Oh c'mon!

[*She runs, opens the back door, and shouts.*]

HEY
WHERE THE HECK ARE YOUR / TEACHERS

OSCAR:
Shelley I got it I'll take care of it

[OSCAR *runs out past her.*]

SHELLEY:
JESUS LOVES YOU
BUT YOU'RE MAKING IT HARD FOR HIM

[*She slams the door. Another rock hits the window. Then another. Then it stops.* SHELLEY *goes back to the vegetables. She starts chopping rather violently. She stops. She breathes. There's a timid knocking on the door.* EMMA *opens the door. She's wearing a scarf on her head.*]

Emma it's great to see you
I was so worried

EMMA:
I'm sorry I had a bunch of appointments
I should have called

SHELLEY:
No no that's fine I'm happy to see you

EMMA:
I'd love to help out today if that's all right

SHELLEY:
Of course it is
How are you feeling

EMMA:
Uh
Well I'm on steroids now so that's kind of messing with me emotionally
But all my counts are up so that's good news

SHELLEY:
If there's anything you need you just ask OK
If your mom needs help I can send food
take you to the hospital . . .

[*A sort of awkward beat between them.*]

EMMA:
Yeah /
I'll tell her

[FROG *enters.*]

FROG:
Oh no!
Your pretty hair!

SHELLEY:
Frog leave her alone

EMMA [*to* FROG]:
Don't worry it's still there
It's just getting kinda stringy

FROG:
Well even with no hair
you are much more attractive
than the person they had serving soup last week

EMMA:
Aw thanks Frog

FROG:
Oh god I hate the thought of them putting you in that
big radiation machine
Have you thought about doing something more holistic

EMMA:
There's no machine
They just use a catheter and pump the chemicals right into me

[*She pulls down her shirt to reveal a bandage covering a port on her upper chest.*]

FROG:
I don't like the looks of that
I think you should look into some holistic methods
I know they're doing some good stuff down in Mexico

SHELLEY:
Sloan Kettering is the best in the country

FROG:
Yeah but this country's out to kill us

SHELLEY:
Frog you need to get out of here it's almost ten

FROG:
I will Shelley I just wanna be supportive OK

SHELLEY:
Tasha's coming at ten and she can't see you in here

FROG:
Loud and clear Shelley

[OSCAR *enters.*]

OSCAR:
Oh hey

FROG:
Emma's back from her chemotherapy

SHELLEY:
Frog!

EMMA:
It's OK I have to tell people at some point

[*Beat.* OSCAR *looks stricken.*]

OSCAR:
Oh
Wow
It's cancer
My mom went through that shit I'm really sorry
I'm going to pray for you

[*Beat.*]

EMMA:
Hey you guys wanna see a picture of my doctor
He's cute he looks kind of like a bald Johnny Depp

[OSCAR *shifts uncomfortably as* EMMA *shows them the photo.*]

FROG:
He's OK I know some handsomer men personally
but I've traveled a lot

EMMA:
And look isn't this nice?
Tons of people sent me flowers

[*She scrolls through her phone.*]

FROG:
What's this one?
Just you in front of the hospital?

EMMA:
Yeah I'm documenting everything I don't know why

FROG:
Gives you a feeling of control in an uncontrollable situation

[*The church bell starts ringing.*]

SHELLEY:
OK Frog you're out
Go!
Go!

FROG:
I'm going Shelley I'm going sheesh

[*He blows a kiss to* EMMA.]

Stay strong

SHELLEY:
Go

[FROG *exits.*]

OSCAR:
I should get back to my

[*Uncomfortable beat.*]

EMMA:
OK
I'll see you

OSCAR:
. . . Yeah

[*He exits.* SHELLEY *notices that something's wrong with* EMMA.]

SHELLEY:
You're sure you feel well enough to work . . .

EMMA:
Yeah
Yeah
I don't need any special treatment
I'm gonna make some kick-ass soup

SHELLEY:
I like your attitude
but if you need a break you have to / speak up

EMMA:
I know

[EMMA *goes to a box and takes out some carrots.*]

SHELLEY:
Hey!
Sorry I'm so sorry I didn't meant to yell
just please don't touch those vegetables without washing your hands

[EMMA *is a little taken aback. She walks over to the sink, washes her hands, and puts on gloves.* SHELLEY *goes to the fridge and starts rummaging around.*]

[EMMA *starts chopping.*]

SHELLEY [*from the fridge*]:
We need extra everything it's getting crazy out there
Almost twice as many guys as last week
pretty soon the whole city's gonna be homeless
It feels like the end of the / world

EMMA:
Ow shit I cut my

SHELLEY:
Are you OK

EMMA:
I cut my finger /
I cut my finger

SHELLEY:
Here c'mon let's put it under the faucet

EMMA:
I cut my finger

[EMMA *starts crying.*]

I cut my finger
I'm fine I'm fine it's not deep

[SHELLEY *holds* EMMA's *finger under the faucet.*]

It's not deep
It's not deep

[EMMA *is sobbing.*]

SHELLEY:
You're OK
Take a deep breath and just count
Count it out
Count from one to twenty

EMMA:
One, two, three, four, five, six

SHELLEY:
Here let me look at it keep counting

EMMA:
Seven, eight, nine

SHELLEY:
You're gonna be fine I promise

[SHELLEY *examines* EMMA's *finger.*]

EMMA:
Ten, eleven, twelve

SHELLEY:
I can't even see the cut
It's like it already healed
It's like a miracle

[EMMA *grabs on tightly to* SHELLEY.]

SCENE NINE

[*Later that same day, after lunch service. The bell rings four times as* OSCAR *carries in a bunch of dishes while pressing his cell phone to his ear with his shoulder.*]

OSCAR:
Estaba bromeando
era una broma estúpida!
Rosa, estoy en el trabajo
no me hagas esto
Voy a llegar a las seis y después salimos
A donde quiere ir

[FROG *enters.*]

¿Que?
Ese no fue lo que dije
Disculpame, pero no es lo que dije
Rosa
Rosa
Rosa
Mierda

[OSCAR *hangs up.*]

FROG:
Hey Oscar

OSCAR:
Hey

FROG:
How can you tell if a man has been having oral sex
with a duck?

OSCAR:
I don't know

[FROG *blows a bunch of white feathers into the air. It's quite beautiful.*]

FROG:
That was for you man you see
That's an English as a Second Language joke

[FROG *exits.* OSCAR *grabs a broom and starts sweeping up the feathers. From the dining room he hears:*]

EMMA:
OSCAR
OSCAR
WE NEED YOU OUT HERE OSCAR

SHELLEY:
OSCAR

OSCAR:
Shit

[*He exits.*]

[*From offstage,* OSCAR *can be heard screaming. This is followed by loud shouts and laughter from* SHELLEY *and* EMMA. EMMA *and* SHELLEY *enter, still laughing, their arms laden with dishes.*]

SHELLEY:
Oh my gosh that was amazing you scared the heck out of him

EMMA:
He screamed like a girl!

OSCAR [*offstage*]:
THAT WAS NOT FUNNY
LADIES YOU ARE NOT FUNNY

SHELLEY:
Oh no
I might pee
I might pee

[EMMA *laughs even harder.*]

No never mind I'm OK I'm fine
I'm not going to pee
Oh man!
His face
Amazing you're amazing
They love you those guys
You bring a lot of light into that situation
and that's not easy believe me

EMMA:
Can I ask you something weird
Do you ever fantasize about washing their feet?

[*Beat.*]

[SHELLEY *starts laughing again.*]

SHELLEY:
Sorry I'm sorry it's

[*She can't stop laughing.*]

No No I do not think about
I don't even like feet

EMMA:
C'mon!
I mean didn't you ever think about stuff like that
when you wanted to become a nun

SHELLEY:
No nope no I did not

EMMA:
OK but what about other stuff
Like couldn't we help them find jobs?

SHELLEY [*sobering up a little*]:
Oh
Uh
That's a great idea but that's not what we do here
We don't have the resources for that

EMMA:
Yeah but it's just phone calls right
Hooking them up with places that are hiring
Helping them find clothes
I could even teach them to make résumés

SHELLEY:
Well you'd need a little money for that
and a whole lot of time
Do you mind passing me that sponge

EMMA:
Would you mind if I did some research

SHELLEY:
No no please do some
research

[SHELLEY *starts scrubbing the pot.*]

[OSCAR *enters.*]

OSCAR:
Hey ladies seriously
You made me look stupid out there and that's not cool
Those guys have to think I'm tough
So if I scream

because someone jumps out of a closet at me
that makes me look bad OK
That makes it harder for me to do my job

SHELLEY:
You're right Oscar we apologize

EMMA:
Yeah we're really sorry

[*Beat.*]

OSCAR:
OK
Thank you

[OSCAR *exits.* EMMA *starts laughing.* SHELLEY *tries not to break but she is beaming at* EMMA.]

EMMA:
So what *did* you think about?

SHELLEY:
What?

EMMA:
When you first wanted to become a nun
What did / you

SHELLEY:
Oh uh
Honestly
I thought about getting back at my mom

EMMA:
Whoa what really

SHELLEY:

Yeah I mean at first that's not why I went through with it obviously
but yeah when I was fifteen I uh
I had to write an essay on a famous feminist
And my mom God rest her soul
she was a famous feminist herself
and a die-hard atheist
(ugh I can't get the crud off the bottom of this pot)
So I wrote my essay on a Catholic feminist
I thought that would really upset her
yet still fulfill the requirements of the course

EMMA:

. . . Your mom was famous?

SHELLEY:

In certain circles
Academia
She wasn't like Gloria Steinem or anything

EMMA:

Oh yeah
Who's Gloria Steinem again?

SHELLEY:

Oh
Wow
Really

[Beat.]

She's a famous feminist

EMMA:

And she's a nun

SHELLEY:
No, no she's not a
I did my report on Dorothy Day

EMMA:
. . .

SHELLEY:
Dorothy Day devoted her life to the homeless
started the *Catholic Worker*
No offense but you were actually in college right

EMMA:
Not that long

SHELLEY:
OK well I'm bringing books and you're going to have to read them

EMMA:
Yeah but why were you so pissed off at your mom

SHELLEY:
Because she married my dad
Who was
Well let's just say he's not the kindest man in the world
and I thought she was a hypocrite for staying with him

[*They are drying now, together.*]

I was fifteen and a little unkind myself

EMMA:
It's funny I always thought people became nuns
because they had like I don't know
Visions
Or like God came to them in the night and was like
"Come with me"

SHELLEY:
Oh that happened too

EMMA:
Wait what

SHELLEY:
Yeah I mean much later but
Ha
It's not that interesting

EMMA:
Oh c'mon
What was it
What was it

SHELLEY:
It was technically more of a dream than a vision

EMMA:
Yeah but what was it

SHELLEY:
Uh
Well
I had this dream about this boy in my school
. . . Rob Kolker

EMMA:
Oooooh

SHELLEY:
Yeah it was not like that OK
He was a junior when I was a freshman
Everyone had a crush on him he wore a cowboy hat
and later he ended up living on a sailboat
Anyway
In the dream I was wearing a dress

I was wearing the dress I wore to my high school prom
and I used to have horrible eczema in high school
Do you know what that is

EMMA:
Yeah like scales

SHELLEY:
Uh yeah
Sort of
So in the dream my eczema
was out of control it manifested as these
huge weeping sores and I
I was awash in shame I felt like an affront to humanity
like how dare I go around offending the world with my

[*She gestures vaguely to her whole self.*]

EMMA:
. . . Scales?

SHELLEY:
Yeah
Or
Not just the scales but all of it

[SHELLEY *gestures again to her whole self.*]

And in my dream I was curled up in Rob Kolker's lap
and he was looking down at me right at my arm
My scaly arm
And I felt a kind of stabbing shame
I wanted to die
I wanted to die
I knew that he must be looking at me with
contempt or disgust or

I was waiting to be annihilated by his disgust
but instead he said . . .

[*Beat.*]

EMMA:
What did he say

SHELLEY:
He said
. . . You are adorable

[*Beat.*]

And he was looking down at me with such gentleness
That I understood I was
Received
in my entirety
weeping sores and all
that my body was not an affront but a
I'm sorry I know this sounds dorky
but I don't have any other words
I understood that my body was holy
that I am holy
And when I woke up
I knew that it was possible to look at myself like this
And at others
With gentleness
With

[*Beat.*]

Adoration

[*Pause.*]

EMMA:
Huh

SHELLEY:
Yeah it's hard to
It loses something in the speaking

EMMA:
But don't you ever want that with someone in real life
I know you have God but sometimes don't you just want Rob Kolker?

[*Beat.*]

SHELLEY:
Sure

[*Making a joke:*]

But you know I have a cat so

EMMA:
Ohhhh
what's its name

SHELLEY:
Pumpkin

EMMA:
Orange?

SHELLEY:
Yup my little niece named him
Sophie I love her like crazy

EMMA:
Yeah I get it I have two nieces and
I love them both so much I could die

SHELLEY:
Ha yes sometimes I feel like I love Sophie
and Pumpkin
so much I could die

[*Long beat.*]

I'm gonna go clean the tables

[SHELLEY *exits.* EMMA *looks after her. Then she picks up a scraper and starts scraping the bottom of a pan. She is working happily.*]

[SHELLEY *reenters.*]

SHELLEY:
Why don't you do some research and
I'll ask Tasha if there are funds
we could put towards a job program

EMMA:
Wait really

SHELLEY:
Yeah why not
She'll probably say no but what the heck

[SHELLEY *exits.*]

SCENE TEN

[*The middle of the night.* EMMA *and* OSCAR *stand facing each other in the darkness.*]

EMMA:
I think I'm sleepwalking

OSCAR:
I am turning on the light OK
I'm turning on the light

[*He turns on the light.*]

EMMA:
Boo!

[*He reacts. She starts laughing.*]

Remember that freaky face
Remember how scared you were by that / freaky face

OSCAR:
Look
I'm really sorry that you're sick
but I can't be talking to you right now
I have a girlfriend
Rosa
I'm in love with Rosa
and I'm going to ask her to be my wife
and we are going to live like this OK
Holding one another up

[OSCAR *makes* FROG's *church gesture with his hands.*]

and so I can't fuck that up
Do you understand I cannot fuck that up

EMMA:
Yeah I totally get it

OSCAR:
Then what are you doing here

EMMA:
I can't sleep I can't sleep anymore
And I'm hungry
You got anything to eat

[*Beat.*]

OSCAR:
Yeah

[*He goes to the fridge.*]

Rosa packed me a late night snack
You can have it I'm not that hungry
Here you go
I'm going to go check the playground and you
can go ahead and eat as much as you / want

EMMA:
You're not going to catch my cancer

OSCAR:
Please don't do this to me

EMMA:
What you can't have a meal with me?
I can't sleep and I
I need some fucking
Human
Company
I'm very alone
I'm very alone
And also I'm dying

I'm dying so fuck you
you didn't run off when I was sucking your cock
and now you can't have a simple human meal with me
Fuck you if you can't have a simple
human meal with me

[*Beat.*]

OSCAR:
Hey look / I

EMMA:
Fuck you

[*He sighs. He starts laying out the food.*]

OSCAR:
C'mon Emma
I'm sorry
Let's eat together
C'mon I'm a jerk

[*She won't eat.*]

Let's have a special human meal

[*She won't look at him.*]

Hey
You know what's delicious is
Clementines

[*He starts peeling it.*]

This Clementine
Mmmmmmm
I wouldn't want to miss out on this
This is sweet
and
delicious

[*Beat.*]

Here one slice c'mon

[*She takes one. She puts it in her mouth.*]

EMMA:
I've had better

OSCAR:
Look I'm sorry I was a jerk . . .

EMMA:
I am a little crazy Oscar

OSCAR:
Yeah I know

EMMA:
No I mean since I've been sick
Everything feels so out of my control
and I can't
I'm sort of following my impulses because
well why not
why not right
And I'm sorry I'm so sorry
I don't want to mess up your relationship with Rosa
but I think I'm going to
Because right now what I want is more important than Rosa

and it's more important than you
And what I want
is for you to feed me another piece of this Clementine OK

OSCAR:
Jesus you're a piece of work

EMMA:
So are you
You are so beautiful Oscar you really are
You're a piece of work

OSCAR:
Oh c'mon stop it I'm a man I'm not beautiful

[*They are holding hands.*]

I mean I'm
. . . guapo

[EMMA *begins to exert a small amount of pressure on* OSCAR'*s hand until she has guided it to the Clementine. She wraps his fingers around it and guides it toward her mouth. He feeds her the Clementine.*]

Oh man

SCENE ELEVEN

[FROG *is showered and wearing new clothes. He holds a bouquet of daisies.* OSCAR *enters.*]

OSCAR:
Hey Hey Papi Shampoo!

FROG:
What the heck does that mean

OSCAR:
Papi Shampoo look at you!
You a ladies man today
"Papi Shampoo" that means like a playa
It means you wash your hair
for the ladies

FROG:
Hey cut it out man

OSCAR:
Why you look so nice Frog?
What you got flowers for you got a lady

FROG:
Nah man
I've been staying somewhere
Emma she hooked me up with a shelter over on Broadway
They've got a shower

OSCAR:
Yeah but who are the flowers for

FROG:
Who do you think dummy
Emma
Emma had her final chemo session today
so I brought her some flowers man
What'd you bring her

OSCAR:
Oh
Uh
I can't encourage her you know that

I'm trying to make things work with Rosa
Emma set up you up good huh?

FROG:
Yes, actually she did
She made some calls on my behalf and now
Well
I've got a job interview

OSCAR:
Wow man that's fantastic

FROG:
Yeah let's not—
Even keel my friend OK
It's just a reception job
I'd be a receptionist at a shelter for the mentally ill
So that's confusing right

OSCAR:
Nah Frog it's great

FROG:
When I was a kid my bubby she worked at a retirement home
taking care of old Jewish ladies
And I always thought it was a little strange
Because she was an old Jewish lady herself
so who was taking care of her?

OSCAR:
Well good luck man

FROG:
Yeah I just gotta try to be consistent
that's going to be the issue
Consistency is not my strong suit
being on time that kind of thing
Plus I have to be on top of the medication so we'll see

[*Beat.*]

OSCAR:
Hey do you think
Do you think those flowers could be from me too

FROG:
What no way my friend no way
Do you know what I had to do to get these flowers

OSCAR:
C'mon please I don't want to look like an asshole

FROG:
No way

[SHELLEY *enters.*]

SHELLEY:
Hey are those for Emma

OSCAR:
Yeah

FROG:
They're from me

SHELLEY:
We can have a little party I brought this cake

OSCAR:
Oh man
I'll be right back

[OSCAR *exits.*]

SHELLEY:
I got candles too is that weird?

FROG:
No way candles are beautiful let's do candles

[*She takes the candles from the bag and hands some to* FROG. *They start putting them on the cake.*]

FROG [*as they're working*]:
Hey Shelley
Ask me if I'm an orange

SHELLEY:
Are you an orange

FROG:
No

SHELLEY:
That's a good one
You look nice today, Frog

FROG:
Emma she set me up with these new duds
and she got me a job interview
It's for next week next Wednesday at 2 P.M.
I don't know if you heard

SHELLEY:
I did hear and I think it's wonderful

FROG:
How come you never set me up, Shelley

SHELLEY:
I don't know
I'm sorry

FROG:
You're smart right you're a really smart girl
Why do you kowtow to authority sister
Why aren't you your own authority
The Catholic Church
C'mon

SHELLEY:
Well you disagree with a lot of the choices
made by this country right
Why do you stay in this country

FROG:
Oh believe me I've tried to make a go of it in other places

SHELLEY:
Right but you came back here

FROG:
OK but I'm saying what's your deal
What are you helping all these losers out for
Why do you care about these losers

SHELLEY:
I'm helping you Frog you're not a loser

FROG:
No way Emma helped me you never helped me

SHELLEY:
Well I have helped you Frog
quite a few times
you might not remember

FROG:
Emma helped me

[Beat.]

SHELLEY:
OK you know what I don't want to argue
this is Emma's / day and I

[EMMA *enters. She looks wrecked.*]

FROG:
Hey! Here's our sunshine!
Look at her
You look great kid how do you feel

[FROG *presents his flowers.*]

These are for you

EMMA:
Oh
Wow
Thanks

FROG:
Shelley got you a cake too but we can wait on that

SHELLEY:
I bet you're exhausted

[EMMA *starts to cry.*]

EMMA:
No I'm fine I'm sorry

FROG:
Oh god I hate to see you cry
you need a joke you want a joke

SHELLEY:
I bet you just need some sleep
Why don't you go home and we'll
celebrate another time

EMMA:
I don't want to go home
I can't be around my mom right now

FROG:
What happened?

EMMA:
We got in this stupid fight because I borrowed some money
I took ten bucks out of her purse
so I could get something to eat on the way to chemo
and she freaked out like I'm some kind of criminal

SHELLEY:
Wait she didn't take you to the hospital
Who took you to the / hospital?

EMMA:
I go by myself
It's worse for me if she comes

FROG:
Hey if your mom is abusive you should stay with Shelley
I mean I'd let you stay at my place but I don't think you qualify
But Shelley you live in an apartment right

SHELLEY:
Uh
Yes I do
Emma I'm happy to have you stay if that would help

FROG:
Oh yeah party at Shelley's

EMMA:
No no I don't need a place to stay

FROG:
Look if your mom's abusive you gotta tell us OK

EMMA:
No I'm fine OK I'm fine
Can we please stop talking / about this

[OSCAR *enters.*]

OSCAR:
Hey Emma
Congratulations
I got you this Bear
Just a little Bear
I wanted to say congratulations so
It's a Jellycat bear

FROG:
Oh yeah they sell those at the Rite Aid

[OSCAR *glares at* FROG.]

EMMA:
Thanks Oscar

[*She takes the Jellycat bear and cradles it.*]

Oh my god I love it so much

SHELLEY:
Why don't we light these candles

FROG:
I got it

[FROG *lights the candles with a Zippo from his pocket.*]

Make a wish

[EMMA *makes a wish. She blows out the candles, but only a few go out.*]

EMMA:
Oh no

SHELLEY:
It's OK you'll still get your / wish

[*Suddenly* FROG *lunges in and grabs all the remaining candles with his bare hand to put out the flame.*]

[EMMA *screams.*]

SHELLEY [*calm*]:   OSCAR:
Frog   Shit!
Give me your hand   Oh man
Give me your hand   Jesus Christ Frog
C'mon let's go to the sink What is wrong with you man

FROG:
What
What

[SHELLEY *holds* FROG's *hand under the faucet.*]

She got her wish

SCENE TWELVE

[SHELLEY *alone on the phone, mid-conversation.*]

SHELLEY:
I apologize I'm not trying to interfere in a family situation
but Emma is welcome to stay with me if that's helpful
Please know that we're here for her and for your whole family
What?

[*Long beat.*]

No I assumed you knew that she was working here
Right
Uh huh
Well that's why I thought it would be helpful
for you and I to—

[*Beat.*]

No she doesn't know I'm calling
I got your number from her emergency contact sheet

[*Long beat.*]

Yes I think we should meet as soon as possible

[OSCAR *enters and lingers by the counter.*]

We're in the Bronx on the corner of 167th and
Yes I can come to you
Let me get a pen

[OSCAR *takes a sandwich out of the fridge. He's conspicuously distracted.*]

Go ahead

[SHELLEY *is writing.*]

Uh huh I'll see you then

[*She hangs up.*]

Have you seen Emma

[*Beat.*]

OSCAR:
What
No
No

SHELLEY:
OK well I have to go out / for a

OSCAR:
Rosa and I broke up

SHELLEY:
Oh no I'm so sorry

OSCAR:
Yeah she uh
Do you have an iPhone 4?

SHELLEY:
Yeah I think so or no it's a 4S

OSCAR:
Yeah but you know what a pass code is right

SHELLEY:
Uh

OSCAR:
It protects your phone so nobody can read your texts or emails
Here I'll show you

[*He takes out his phone and starts showing her.*]

See my phone is locked right now
so you can't read my private things
And then I put in my code
and there I can see everything

SHELLEY:
Uh huh

OSCAR:
But the iPhone 4 has a little uh
The thing about these dudes in California
I think a lot of them don't have girlfriends
They're computer guys so they don't have girlfriends
and so they didn't test this pass code feature carefully
You know what I'm saying?
Watch this:
See this is my camera OK
OK you see that

SHELLEY:
Yup

OSCAR:
And even though the phone is locked
The camera icon still appears for some reason
and when I press the icon it opens right up to my camera
and then Shelley look at this!

I am in the phone
I am in the phone
pass code does not protect me

SHELLEY:
I'm not sure I

OSCAR:
You know how I figured out this little problem?
I didn't
Rosa figured it out
Rosa figured it out
She figured it out and she read all my texts
and now I'm dead I'm a dead man!

[OSCAR *is overcome by his shitty situation.*]

SHELLEY:
Are you saying that Rosa read something
You didn't want her to read?

OSCAR [*not looking up*]:
Yeah that crazy girl she texted me

[*Beat.*]

SHELLEY:
Emma?

OSCAR:
Yeah I don't know why but she texted me some wild shit
and Rosa I think she misunderstood
because this stuff she texted me / was out of control

SHELLEY:
You know what I need to go and this none of my business

OSCAR:
Wait are you pissed are you pissed at me?

SHELLEY:
No no I'm not I just have to go meet someone
So I'd rather not be talking to you about this right now

OSCAR:
You're lying you're pissed you look pissed

SHELLEY:
Yeah well maybe I am but not at you
I'm just going through some stuff too
Oscar

OSCAR:
Oh man Shelley I'm sorry what is it

SHELLEY:
Never mind

OSCAR:
Come on I mean we're friends right you can / tell me

SHELLEY:
I'll see you tomorrow

OSCAR:
Please don't stay mad at me

SHELLEY:
I'm not mad at you I just told you that

OSCAR:
Yeah but
are you disappointed in me

[Beat.]

SHELLEY:
Yes actually
I am a little disappointed in you

[*Long beat.*]

But I'll get over it

SCENE THIRTEEN

[SHELLEY *and* EMMA *sitting in the kitchen.* EMMA's *head is uncovered. She wears her hair like she did in the first scene.*]

[*Long pause.*]

EMMA:
It just came out of my mouth
and then once I said it I couldn't take it back
And the more I kept pretending
the more it started to feel true to me
it was kind of a relief
like thank God now I can stop pretending that I'm OK all the time
It's like the outside finally made sense with the inside
I'm sorry it sounds so stupid when I say it out loud
but I *feel* like I have cancer

SHELLEY:
Right but you don't

EMMA:
I mean on the inside

SHELLEY:
Real cancer happens on the inside

EMMA:
Right but I'm saying it felt true / to me

SHELLEY:
No I'm sorry that's not acceptable

EMMA:
So what you think I'm what evil?

SHELLEY:
What
No
No I don't think you're evil I think that you lied
You lied about something very big

EMMA:
But you're a nun aren't you / supposed to

SHELLEY:
You told me your mother abused you

EMMA:
I never said that Frog said it

SHELLEY:
Did your mother abuse you

EMMA:
No not physically / but

SHELLEY:
What emotionally psychologically
welcome to the club

EMMA:
I don't know I can't explain it!

SHELLEY:
Did your mother abuse you?

EMMA:

No, no not exactly it's just that I uh

SHELLEY:

You just *feel* like she did

EMMA:

No that's not what I / said

SHELLEY:

Because from what I can tell your mother loves you like crazy
She's working two jobs to put you through college

EMMA:

I know that!

SHELLEY:

And this isn't the first time right
This is a pattern your mother told me this / is a

EMMA:

Yes /
Yes

SHELLEY:

You never went to college
She paid for your whole first semester
and you never even went to / class

EMMA:

I was depressed I couldn't get out of bed

[*Beat.*]

There's something wrong with me and no one can even see it
And I don't understand how I'm supposed to go on living
when I'm in all this pain and no one can even see it
It's like I've been through a fucking war or something

SHELLEY:
Please stop it's offensive comparing your / pain to

EMMA:
I'm sorry I'm not comparing
I thought you were supposed to be compassionate

[*The bell rings four times.*]

SHELLEY:
Emma I need to start dinner
I appreciate you coming up here to talk to me in person
that was brave
But I don't think it would be right
for you to continue working here

EMMA:
What

SHELLEY:
You need to take some time to figure this out with your family
with the people who love you
Your mom and I talked and she's going to find someone for you
a psychologist or / a

EMMA:
HELP ME

[*Beat.*]

I'm sorry I'm sorry I yelled

SHELLEY:
I have to do the responsible thing Emma
There are a lot of people who depend on me here
to get them through the day
You have a family who loves you

who is ready to get you the help that you need
OK
There are a lot of smart people out there who can help you figure this out
but I am not one of them

EMMA:
Please forgive me Shelley

[SHELLEY *is paralyzed for a moment.*]

You can't even look at me
You can forgive everyone else in this whole stupid world
except for me

SHELLEY:
I'm not qualified to help you Emma

EMMA:
You're a nun
I mean if a nun isn't qualified to
love
to forgive
then what the fuck am I supposed to do
HELP ME
HELP ME
HELP / ME

[OSCAR *comes running in.*]

OSCAR:
What the heck
What happened
Are you ladies all right?

[EMMA *runs into his arms.*]

Hey whoa
whoa
You're all right

SHELLEY:
I'm calling your mom Emma

OSCAR:
What's going on

SHELLEY:
She doesn't have cancer

[*Beat.*]

OSCAR:
You're clean?

EMMA:
Well yeah but

[OSCAR *shouts in joy.*]

OSCAR:
That's fantastic

[*He picks* EMMA *up off the ground.*]

Thank you / God

EMMA:
No no no no Oscar stop put me / down it's

OSCAR:
Yeah it's too much I understand it's a lot of emotion

SHELLEY:
No no it's not it's not a lot of emotion!
Emma tell him
You should tell / him yourself

OSCAR:
What tell me / what

[*Long beat.* EMMA *is too ashamed to say it.*]

SHELLEY:
. . . She lied

OSCAR:
What

SHELLEY:
She never had cancer she lied

OSCAR:
Oh

[*Long beat.*]

That's weird

EMMA:
Yeah
Yes
I don't know why I
It was my first day and I felt like Shelley was judging me

SHELLEY:
Wait what are you blaming me now?

EMMA:
No no I'm not saying it's your fault
I take responsibility I do

I can't handle the thought that
someone might be mad at me or might not like me

OSCAR:
But you were
You had like the thing on your chest
For the chemo

EMMA:
I did that myself I got some gauze and
I'm sorry oh my god I'm / so sorry

OSCAR:
You brought pictures

EMMA:
Those were real!
He was my doctor when I was fifteen
and I had my appendix out and everybody sent me flowers

[Beat.]

He really was my doctor

[Pause.]

OSCAR:
OK
Uh
I don't understand what's going on
But you definitely don't have cancer right?

EMMA:
I don't have cancer

[Beat.]

OSCAR:
So that's something to be thankful for
I'm happy for you because no one deserves cancer
My mom went through it and it was terrible
So I'm going to knock on some wood for you

[*He walks over to the counter. He knocks on wood. He exits.*]

SHELLEY:
You should go Emma I need to / start the

EMMA:
What if I
If I start seeing a psychologist
Could I keep working here if I see a psychologist
Like you said

[*Beat.*]

Please I respect whatever decision you make
but working here is the only good I have done in my life
I've done good here you know that I've done good

SHELLEY:
. . . Yes you have

EMMA:
Maybe you could let me stay for a trial period
I'll do extra work around here whatever you want

SHELLEY:
. . . I would need to think really hard about that

EMMA:
Please look at me with gentleness

SHELLEY:
What

EMMA:
Please look at me with whatever you said
With adoration

[*Beat.*]

SHELLEY:
If you want to stay for the afternoon I could use the help
And I think you should tell the guys yourself

EMMA:
Yes absolutely

SHELLEY:
. . . Why don't you go out and wipe down the tables

EMMA:
Thank you

SHELLEY:
You're welcome

[EMMA *goes to the closet and gets spray and rag. She exits.* SHELLEY *keeps prepping for a few moments, then walks over to the microwave.*]

I know that I may not be looking at this situation
with much clarity
I have been lied to so many times in my life that I'm
having a hard time trusting myself here

[*Long pause.*]

She's one of the poor right?
That's why she's here

[*The microwave buzzes.* SHELLEY *just stands there for a few moments.*]

[FROG *enters.*]

FROG:
Hey Shelley

SHELLEY:
Oh hey / Frog

FROG:
Emma told me she told me and I just want to say
What a stupid asshole that girl is

SHELLEY:
Ha
Well
Yes

FROG:
But you should let her stay

SHELLEY:
Frog this is none of your / business

FROG:
People are fucked up Shelley
Angels and assholes
Me for example I'm an asshole but I've got a good heart
and she's done so much around here
Shelley
Shelley
I'm going on two more job interviews next week
Emma did that

SHELLEY:
I know she did

FROG:

This fucked up thing she did is mysterious
but she's a nineteen-year-old girl and that's a mysterious type of person
And she didn't hurt anyone not really
I mean if she was your kid you'd have to forgive her right
and isn't she your kid Shelley
Look at your vocation I would say that she's your kid

SHELLEY:

I don't know if that's how I interpret my vocation
Frog
but I hear you
I have a lot of work to do in here

FROG:

Oh yeah I know
I just wanted to advocate
Just know she has an advocate

SHELLEY:

I hear you

[FROG *exits.* SHELLEY *dumps out a huge bag of potatoes. She starts chopping. After a bit,* EMMA *enters and returns her cleaning supplies to the closet.* EMMA *stands there for a moment looking at* SHELLEY.]

Do you mind helping me with these potatoes

SCENE FOURTEEN

[*Three months later. The sounds of loud, cheerful conversation in the dining room.* SHELLEY *enters in a fall coat, carrying a package. She sets it down and goes to the microwave.*]

SHELLEY:
Please guide me
I uh
I know that I need to say good-bye to let him go with kindness
Whatever his faults he's my father and I owe him that
Seventy times seven
I know that's what you're asking of me but how do I do it

Please give me the words
Help me to love with understanding and without understanding
to love blindly
and foolishly
Amen

[EMMA *enters. She is dressed in an official apron and sensible cloth-ing, much like* SHELLEY *was in the first scene. She looks very grown-up.* SHELLEY *smiles at her.*]

How's it going out there
How are your volunteers

EMMA:
They suck but they're getting it done
Also we're low on bread again
I think we should double the order next week

SHELLEY:
I'll check the budget but I can't make any promises
You need help out there?
I don't have to prep dinner for another hour

EMMA:
We could use a hand with clean up if you don't mind
There's a bunch of families today
Little kids it's depressing

[*As* SHELLEY *grabs cleaning supplies,* FROG *enters. He is dressed up. He holds a potato to his ear.*]

FROG:
Good afternoon Bronx Community Residence and Mental Health
    Facility
Good afternoon Bronx Community Residence
and Mental Health Facility
Uh

SHELLEY:
Hey Frog

[*He shushes her with his hand.* SHELLEY *exits.*]

FROG:
Good afternoon Bronx Community Residence
and Mental Health Facility
Uh
Uh

EMMA:
How may I help you

FROG:
How may I help you

EMMA:
I don't know because I'm totally crazy!

FROG:
Well OK then
You know what you should do if you're totally crazy
You should come and meet with one of our trained social workers

EMMA:
Keep going

FROG:
We provide
Transitional services for those
Transitioning
That can't be right it's redundant

EMMA:
It sounds fine they get the picture

[SHELLEY *reenters from the cafeteria with an armful of dishes and sets them down.*]

SHELLEY:
There really are a lot of them wow

FROG:
Bunch of pigs

SHELLEY:
You look so handsome Frog

FROG:
Yeah I know
Today's my first day I start at five and I can't mess it up
It took me a million interviews to get this job
I gotta show up with the goods

SHELLEY:
I know you've got the goods
They're going to love you
Hey Emma can you be in charge of tomorrow's list

[SHELLEY'*s phone starts ringing.*]

EMMA:
Absolutely can I experiment

SHELLEY:
Sure but no cilantro it weirds me out

[*On the phone:*] Hey Sophie how's Grandpa

[*As she exits:*] Yep I'll be out tomorrow just let me know what you need

[FROG *goes right back to practicing.*]

FROG:
Hi thanks for holding
We're located at
We're located at
Jesus my mind
my mind is totally shot
Sometime around 1974 the atomic bomb went off in there
and now it's a radiated field
How the hell can I do this when I've got no memory

EMMA:
It's on 5670 Riverdale

FROG:
5670 Riverdale

EMMA:
Try it again

FROG:
56
oh god

EMMA:
It's easy Frog:
5, 6, 7 that's all in a row and then you go back to zero
Plus you've got a memory if you can remember 1974

FROG:
Yeah but that's the last year I remember
Or maybe I'm just hungry

EMMA:
You want a sandwich?

FROG:
Nah I think I gotta stop for a while
This is too heady for me I'd rather clean tables

EMMA:
Go for it

[FROG *goes to the closet and grabs some cleaner and a rag. He exits.*
EMMA *continues cleaning. Contentedly.*]

[*After a few moments,* SHELLEY *enters.*]

SHELLEY:
Can I talk to you for a second

EMMA:
OK

SHELLEY:
Uh
Your work here
Over the past few months has been terrific
You've made changes here that I never even
imagined were possible
And if you're interested
Tasha and I would love to put you on salary

[*Pause.* EMMA *just looks at her, stunned.*]

. . . I mean you should take all the time you need
to think about it
Are you OK

EMMA:
Yes oh my god thank you yes

SHELLEY:
Oh good OK you scared me for a second
I thought you were going to say no

EMMA:
No no I mean yes I'd love to have a real job here

SHELLEY:
Great I'm so relieved
Tasha will deal with all the paperwork and uh
she'll have to train you too sorry
I just found out that I have to fly to California for a week or so

EMMA:
Oh wow

SHELLEY:
Yeah my dad
He's been moved to hospice
Finally

EMMA:
I'm sorry

SHELLEY:
Thank you I'm hoping he and I can
Well I'm not sure what I'm hoping
But I think I'm ready to say good-bye

EMMA:
Can I help at all
Do you need anything

SHELLEY:
You know what yes I wanted to ask
Would you be willing to take care of my place while I'm gone
Look after Pumpkin, water my plants

EMMA:
Of course whatever you need

SHELLEY:
Oh that's wonderful thank you
You're welcome to stay there too
I know Pumpkin would love the company
If you don't mind playing with him and petting him a lot
He's a very spoiled cat
Why don't you stop by when we're done here
And I can show you how he likes things

EMMA:
Ha
Sure

SHELLEY:
Oh and in terms of this place
Tasha will be officially in charge of the kitchen
while I'm gone so

EMMA:
. . . Oh
I thought you might put me in charge

SHELLEY:
I think it's a little soon for that

EMMA:
I know I'm sorry I'll just miss you

[OSCAR *enters.*]

Hey Oscar

OSCAR:
Hey
Just here to get my leftovers

[*He opens the refrigerator, grabs his leftovers, and leaves.*]

EMMA:
Do you think he'll ever talk to me again?

SHELLEY:
Give him time

[*Beat.*]

Hey
Look at this

[SHELLEY *pulls a nun's habit out of a huge plastic bag.*]

EMMA:
What is that
Is that a nun dress?

SHELLEY:
Well yes but more importantly
it's a basketball dress

EMMA:
Whoa no way

SHELLEY:
Oh yeah
I don't know if you know this about me Emma
I was the leading point guard in Northern California
Triple A ball

and when I get through all of this
I am heading across the street and I am going to dominate those girls

[EMMA *starts laughing.*]

EMMA:
Ha
Yes I will be there

SHELLEY:
I am going to ruin those girls

SCENE FIFTEEN

[EMMA *is alone in the kitchen, blasting music. She chops vegetables and throws them violently into the soup. She pulls some spices down from above the stove and starts adding them to the pot.* OSCAR *enters.*]

OSCAR:
HEY

EMMA:
OH HEY YOU'RE TALKING TO ME NOW

OSCAR:
OH C'MON DON'T BE LIKE THAT
HOW'S IT GOING HERE WITH TASHA

EMMA:
I FUCKING HATE TASHA BUT SHE'S GONE TODAY

[*She turns down the music.*]

It's all fine
Tasha's fine

OSCAR:
No she's not she's scary
I'm sorry you have to deal with that

EMMA:
Me too it's like penal servitude here now
Whatever I can take it

OSCAR:
We need Shelley man

EMMA:
Yeah no shit
She's gotta stay longer
I don't know what's going on
but her family sounds crazy

OSCAR:
Oh man poor Shelley

EMMA:
Yeah and poor me
I'm going insane here without her

OSCAR:
Yeah
Yeah

[Beat.]

Soup smells good

EMMA:
I'm trying out some new stuff
Fennel

OSCAR:
Cool

[Beat.]

Listen
I want to tell you
Uh
I mean I know I don't need to tell you this
but I want everything to be out in the open
so I want to tell you that I asked Rosa to marry me

[Beat.]

EMMA:
Good for you

OSCAR:
Yeah
Yeah
And she said yes

EMMA:
That's fantastic

OSCAR:
Yeah it is right?
And listen to be clear
I didn't tell her everything about us
but I did have to tell her some things you know because of the texts
which I realize you had every right to send
I realize that I was equally responsible for what happened
and you had a right to send those texts
and I'm sorry that Rosa saw them but that is not your fault

[Beat.]

Are you OK

EMMA:
Yeah
I hope you'll be super happy

OSCAR:
Thank you

[*Pause.*]

So to be clear
I'm not
Except for telling you this
I'm not supposed to talk to you

[*Beat.*]

EMMA:
. . . OK

OSCAR:
Yeah
So

EMMA:
So see ya

[*Pause.*]

OSCAR:
Oh c'mon Emma
You knew I had a girlfriend when / you

EMMA:
Please stop talking to me
You're not supposed to talk to me
I'm a piece of shit and you're not supposed to / talk to me

OSCAR:
Stop it you're an amazing girl and I have real admiration
for how you turned your life around
and I'm just trying to do the same I'm trying to make a life / with Rosa

EMMA:
Jesus I get it just leave me alone

OSCAR:
I'm sorry I'm just trying to say
that you're a beautiful girl or you know woman
human being and I / really wish

EMMA:
Oh my god can you please
Can you please just
GET THE FUCK OUT OF HERE

[*She turns the music back up. She goes back to chopping.* OSCAR *stands there for a moment watching her. He exits.* EMMA *chops. She cuts her finger.*]

Shit
Shit
Shit

[*She runs to the faucet and puts it under water. She stands there and silently counts to twenty. She takes off her apron, goes to the soup, turns it down to a simmer and walks out the door.*]

SCENE SIXTEEN

[SHELLEY *alone in the kitchen sobbing. She tries to recover when* OSCAR *enters.*]

OSCAR:
Shelley girl are you OK
Hey c'mon Shelley

[*She starts crying again.* OSCAR *grabs her some paper towels and hands them to her. He pours her a glass of water.*]

Here
Here
Drink this
C'mon Shelley
Drink this

[*She drinks.*]

Man you were thirsty
You OK?
Shelley you OK?

[SHELLEY *nods.*]

SHELLEY:
Has Emma been in yet

OSCAR:
What no
She ditched us while you were out of town
Tasha's been working by herself for a week
We haven't heard from Emma

SHELLEY:
She uh
She didn't feed my cat

[*Beat.*]

OSCAR:
She didn't feed your

[SHELLEY *starts to cry again.*]

Oh shit

SHELLEY:
He must have thought
He thought I abandoned him
The whole apartment was
He had torn up the whole apartment
looking for food
and water
He shit all over the place he just died there
desperate
Thinking I'd abandoned him
Why didn't you
Why didn't you
Why the fuck didn't anyone call me

OSCAR:
Shelley

SHELLEY:
You or
Tasha why didn't you why didn't you call me
If Emma didn't come to work for a week
Why didn't you call me
I was
I had a lot to deal with
I didn't check in because
I had a lot to
My fucking dad was dying
Oh my god

He didn't have any water
He didn't have any fucking / water

[FROG *enters.*]

FROG:
Hey you guys
Hey Shelley
What's going on
Are you OK Shelley
You need a joke
You wanna hear a joke

OSCAR:
Hey man c'mon give her some space

FROG:
Hey Shelley two penguins are sitting in a bathtub

OSCAR:
C'mon leave her alone she's having a hard day

FROG [*fairly calm at first*]:
Oh yeah I know me too you know why?
There's a fucking government guy following me
oh yeah
oh yeah
He's about 5'9"
very nondescript
that's the kind of guy the CIA sends
the kind of guy that blends right in think I won't notice
fuck you motherfuckers

OSCAR:
Frog man what's going on why aren't you at work

FROG:
Because they know where I work now Oscar
They've got their people disguised in the waiting room

OSCAR:
Hey did you forget your medication
Did you take your medication today

FROG:
Can you look outside and see if he's there
He's wearing a tie
He's wearing a tie just like this one
Because you know what they do
They mock you
They mock you
Throw it back in your face
Look at you sucker working a fucking desk job
Look at what the fuck you are
A nothing
A nothing

OSCAR:
Hey calm down OK
Can you hand me your bag
I'm gonna find you some / medication

[OSCAR *grabs for* FROG's *bag and* FROG *suddenly turns on him, trying to wrestle the bag out of* OSCAR's *hands.*]

FROG:
DON'T TOUCH MY SHIT
DON'T TOUCH MY SHIT ASSHOLE

SHELLEY:
FROG
CALM DOWN

[*Beat.*]

FROG:
. . . OK

SHELLEY:
Listen to me Frog
I'm gonna go check
and see if that CIA dude is still out there
OK
And if he's out there
I'm going to deal with him

[*Beat.*]

FROG:
Thanks
Shelley

[*She gets up and walks out the back door and shuts it.* FROG *watches after her anxiously.*]

OSCAR:
Hey man
I didn't mean to scare you

[SHELLEY *walks back in.*]

FROG:
Was he out there

SHELLEY:
Yeah
He was out there

FROG [*to* OSCAR]:
I told you!

SHELLEY:
I said he needed to leave you alone
I told him if the CIA didn't back off
We were gonna sue their asses
And take them for everything they've got
And he got scared
And he agreed to leave

FROG:
He did

SHELLEY:
Yes he did
So you're safe Frog
You're safe
And I want you to drink some water OK
Oscar can you get him a cup

OSCAR:
Sure

SHELLEY [*as she digs through* FROG'*s bag*]:
We've taken care of the CIA guy
And now we're gonna get you back to your house
OK
We're gonna get you back to your living situation

[*Beat.*]

FROG:
Yeah
OK
Thanks Shelley

SHELLEY:
And can I look through your bag Frog?
Can I see if you have some medication

that might help you sleep?
Because I think after all they've put you through
you deserve to rest

[FROG *nods.*]

FROG:
Yeah
Yeah
I do deserve to rest
Oh man
It's so hot in here

SHELLEY:
Hey Oscar
Can you bring me a cold washcloth

OSCAR:
Sure

SHELLEY [*pulling a pill container out of* FROG'*s bag*]:
OK I found these Frog
This is your Olanzapine
It's gonna help you deal with the stress
caused by these motherfuckers OK

FROG:
Yeah
Yeah
You're sure they're not tampered with

SHELLEY:
Nope this is a clean supply
I've checked them
It's a clean supply

[FROG *takes the pill and puts it in his mouth. He takes a drink of the water.* OSCAR *hands* SHELLEY *the cloth.*]

There you go you got it
And let's cool you off OK
Will you let me touch your face

FROG:
. . . Yeah

[FROG *lets* SHELLEY *wash his face. He relaxes.*]

SHELLEY:
There you go

FROG:
Shit they're evil you know

SHELLEY:
I know
They are evil
and I'm sorry I'm so sorry you have to deal with this
You don't deserve any of this

SCENE SEVENTEEN

[EMMA *is waiting alone in the kitchen for* SHELLEY. *After a bit,* SHELLEY *enters with an armful of dirty dishes. She is dressed in a contemporary nun's habit. A knee-length skirt and jacket. A modest headpiece. She stops and looks at* EMMA. *Her expression is open and generous.*]

EMMA:
Thank you for seeing me

[SHELLEY *nods.*]

I uh
I'm going back to school
upstate
and I didn't want to leave
without apologizing in person

SHELLEY:
All right

[*Beat.*]

EMMA:
Oscar said
He said you were leaving the church
but you're dressed like / a

SHELLEY:
I am leaving
This
costume
was a last ditch effort to make it work
I'm formally leaving tomorrow but until then

[*Beat.*]

I'm still giving it my all

EMMA:
What will you do

[SHELLEY *smiles.*]

SHELLEY:
I . . . have no idea

[EMMA *stares at her, confused and overcome with remorse.*]

It was a decision I would have come to
Eventually
Though your actions were clarifying

EMMA:
I'm sorry I am so / sorry

SHELLEY:
Emma I know that what you did
wasn't actively malicious
I know that you didn't deliberately starve and
Torture
another living creature
who was depending on you for survival

EMMA:
Did you
My letter did you get / my

SHELLEY:
I read it yes thank you
I've been reading it for the past month
I've read it maybe a hundred times
looking for some kind of . . .

[*Beat.*]

And the thing is
I empathize with you Emma
With your
Depression—you said you ran away because you were very
Depressed
and I understand that I do

I realize this might come as a surprise to you
but I have also experienced quite a lot of depression
in my thirty-nine years

[*Long beat.*]

And even though I know that you were in pain
And that what you did was thoughtless
And not
actively malicious
I still believe with all my heart that it was evil

[*Beat.*]

EMMA:
What

SHELLEY:
It was evil and I'm relieved that tomorrow
I will finally be rid of

[*She gestures vaguely to her habit.*]

Whatever obligation this gives me to forgive you

[*The church bell rings three times.*]

I need to finish cleaning up

EMMA:
Shelley I promise you that one day
I will be a different kind of person
a better kind of person
and even though I know this is something

I can never make right I'm going to devote my life to it anyway
and I'm sorry I'm sorry I know I don't deserve it
but I hope that one day you'll be able to forgive me

SHELLEY:
Emma I believe you
I believe that one day you will be
a different kind of person
a better kind of person
and I even believe that one day
I might be able to forgive you
but the thing is

[*Long beat.*]

I don't want to

[*Beat.*]

. . . I feel lighter
and freer
and strangely
. . . happy?
standing here right now knowing that
I don't ever have to forgive you
Ever
Ever
Ever
Ever
Ever
I don't wish you any harm Emma
but if I never forgive you that will be fine with me
I can live with that

[SHELLEY *is looking at* EMMA *with great gentleness.*]

EMMA [*after a bit*]:
Shelley I . . .
I should go

SHELLEY:
Yes

[SHELLEY *lets* EMMA *go.*]

[EMMA *exits.*]

[SHELLEY *looks after* EMMA *for a moment and then, finally, allows herself to relax. Suddenly so much seems possible. She is filled with increasing elation, and eventually something resembling joy.*]